THE LLAMA
AN OFF-COLOR ADULT COLORING BOOK

Honey Badger

ISBN-13: 978-1540500526
ISBN-10: 1540500527

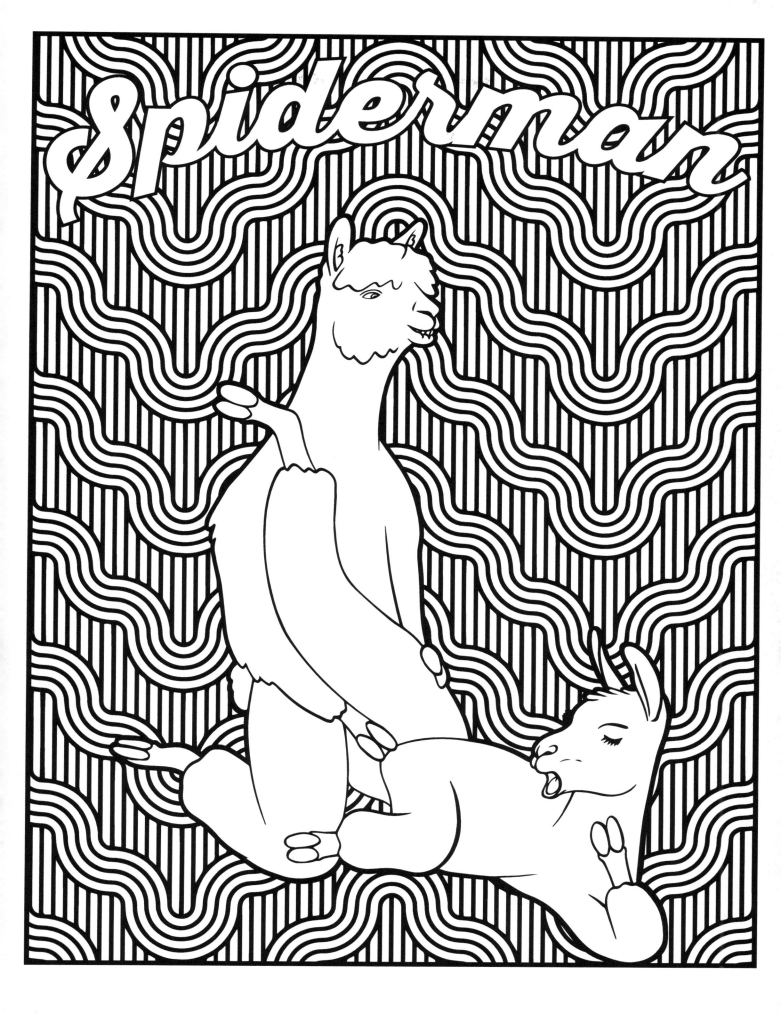

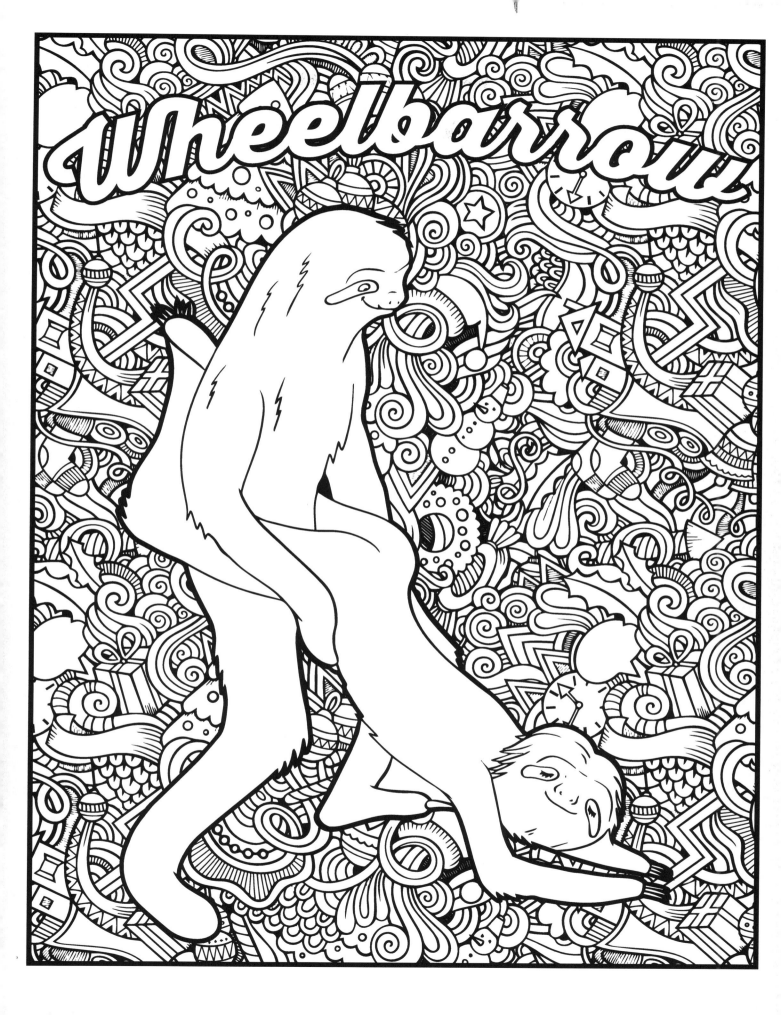

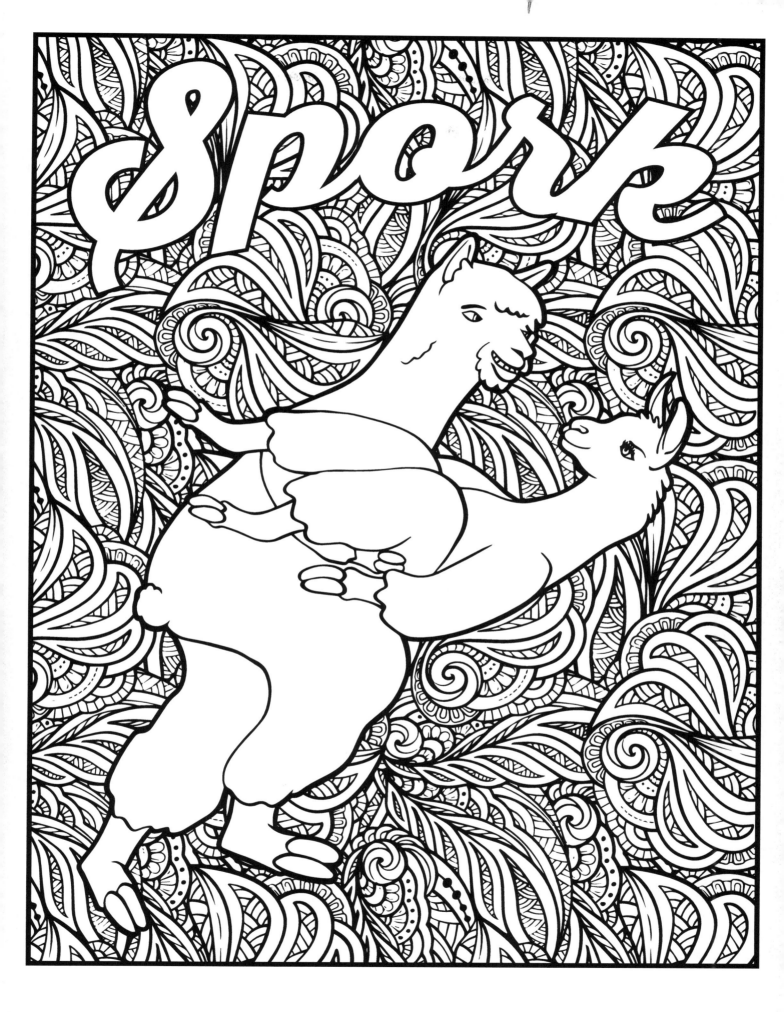

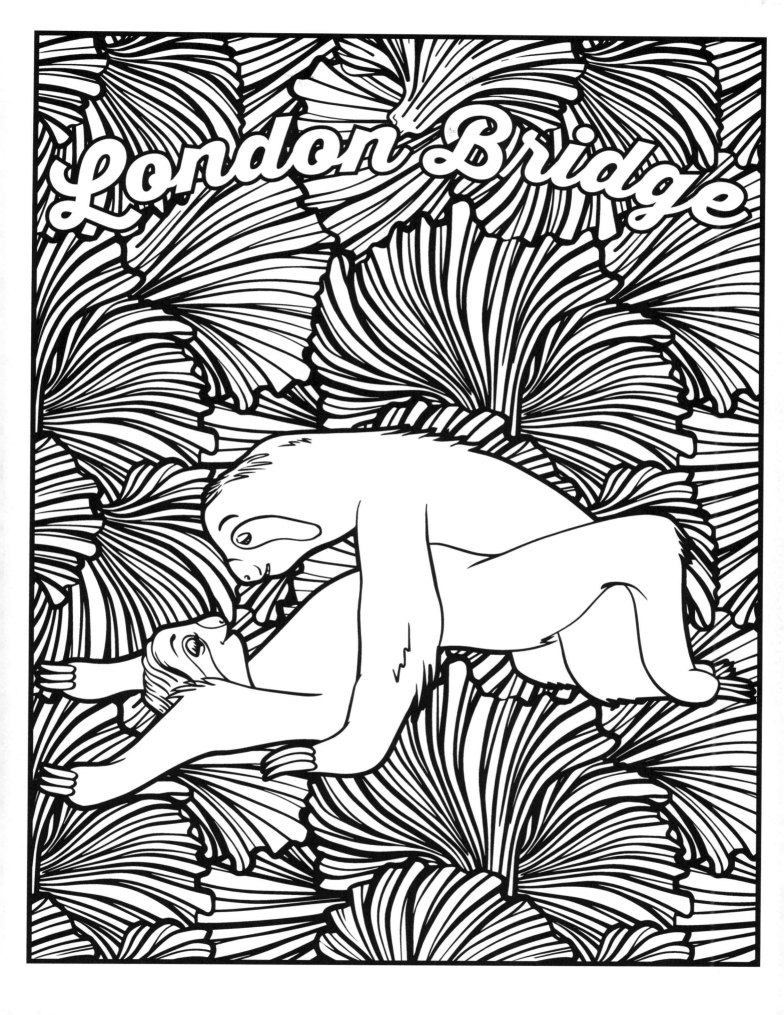

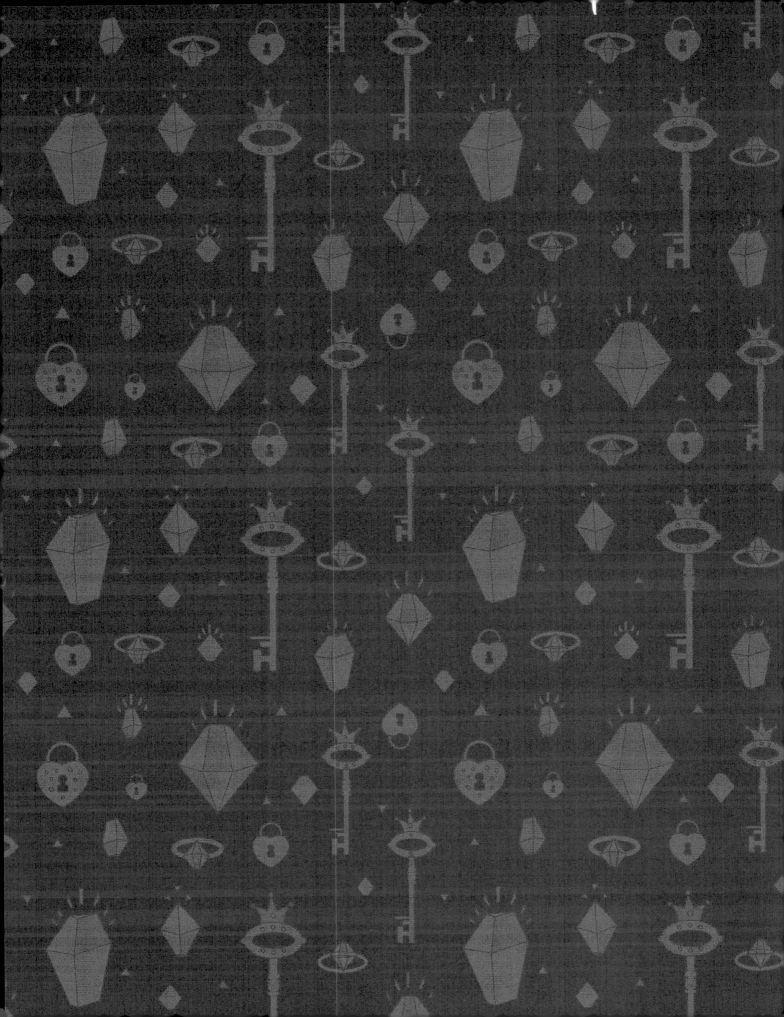

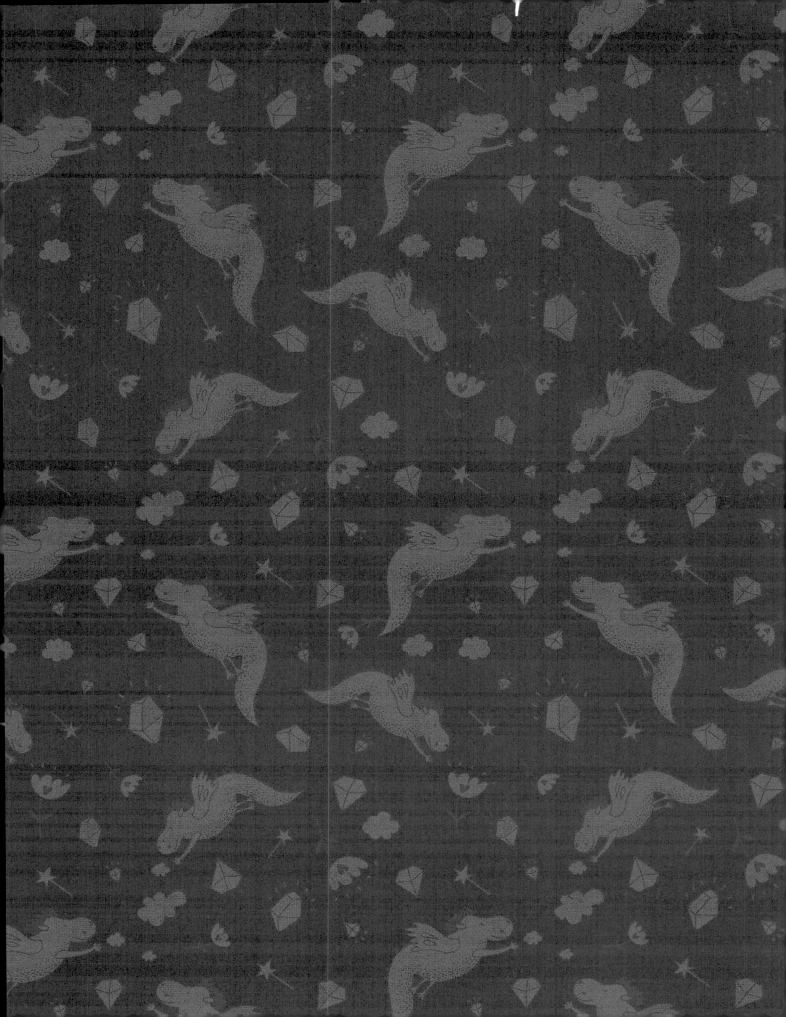

BE SURE TO FOLLOW US
ON SOCIAL MEDIA FOR THE
LATEST GIVEAWAYS & DISCOUNTS

[Instagram] @honeybadgercoloring

[Facebook] Honey Badger Coloring

[Twitter] @badgercoloring

ADD YOURSELF TO OUR MONTHLY
NEWSLETTER FOR FREE DIGITAL
DOWNLOADS AND DISCOUNT CODES

www.honeybadgercoloring.com/newsletter

CHECK OUT OUR OTHER BOOKS!

www.honeybadgercoloring.com

73307189R00044

Made in the USA
Lexington, KY
08 December 2017